Don't Blame It On The Boots

C000226370

A comedy

N. J. Warburton

Samuel French – London
New York – Sydney – Toronto – Hollywood

© 1987 by N. J. Warburton

1.   *This play is fully protected under the Copyright Laws of the British Commonwealth of Nations, the United States of America and all countries of the Berne and Universal Copyright Conventions.*

2.   *All rights, including Stage, Motion Picture, Radio, Television, Public Reading, and Translation into Foreign Languages, are strictly reserved.*

3.   **No part of this publication may lawfully be reproduced in ANY form or by any means - photocopying, typescript, recording (including video-recording), manuscript, electronic, mechanical, or otherwise - or be transmitted or stored in a retrieval system, without prior permission.**

4.   Rights of Performance by Amateurs are controlled by Samuel French Ltd, 52 Fitzroy Street, London W1P 6JR, and they, or their authorized agents, issue licences to amateurs on payment of a fee. **It is an infringement of the Copyright to give any performance or public reading of the play before the fee has been paid and the licence issued.**

5.   Licences are issued subject to the understanding that it shall be made clear in all advertising matter that the audience will witness an amateur performance; that the names of the authors of the plays shall be included on all announcements and on all programmes; and that the integrity of the author's work will be preserved.

   The Royalty Fee indicated below is subject to contract and subject to variation at the sole discretion of Samuel French Ltd.

          Basic fee for each and every
             perfomance by amateurs   Code D
          in the British Isles

   In Theatres or Halls seating Six Hundred or more the fee will be subject to negotiation.

   In Territories Overseas the fee quoted above may not apply. A fee will be quoted on application to our local authorized agent, or if there is no such agent, on application to Samuel French Ltd, London.

6.   The Professional Rights in this play are controlled by David Higham Associates Ltd, 5-8 Lower John Street, Golden Square, London W1R 4HA.

ISBN 0 573 12086 2

DON'T BLAME IT ON THE BOOTS

First performed by SUDS (Stapleford Umbrella Drama Society) on 8th March, 1986, with the following cast of characters.

Ophelia	Alison Rose
Kate	Ina Crouch
Eric	Nick Warburton
Liz	Carol Tomson

Produced by Jenni Sinclair

The publication of this play does not imply that it is necessarily available for performance by amateurs or professionals, either in the British Isles or Overseas. Amateurs and professionals considering a production are strongly advised in their own interests to apply to the appropriate agents for consent before starting rehearsals or booking a theatre or hall.

CHARACTERS

Eric, forty
Liz, thirty-five
Kate, forty
Ophelia, seventeen
Stage Manager
Stage Hands

SYNOPSIS OF SCENES

Scene 1   On stage during late rehearsals for a production of
            Hamlet
Scene 2   On stage. Eight days later, after the first performance
            of *Hamlet*
Scene 3   The dressing-room. The following night

Time——the present

DON'T BLAME IT ON THE BOOTS*

Scene 1

On stage during late rehearsals for a production of Hamlet

Two flats, with a gap C between them, represent castle walls. One is draped with a cloth as if it is still being painted. There is rehearsal clutter dotted about - coffee mugs, coats, pots of paint, etc., a pile of footwear DR, and a couple of chairs

When the CURTAIN *rises Ophelia, young, pretty and earnest, is in Elizabethan costume and sits studying a copy of* Hamlet *in the shadows at the back of the stage*

Music. A pool of light comes up R

Liz enters with a bag containing the pair of boots. She is about thirty and casually dressed. She is about to place the bag with a pile of other footwear, when she takes the boots out, looks at them fondly for a moment and returns them to the bag before leaving

The music fades. General lighting comes up

Kate, the director, is at the back of the auditorium. She is about

---

*NB. Paragraph 3 on page ii of this Acting Edition regarding photocopying and video-recording should be carefully read.

forty, slightly harrassed and inclined to be sarcastic. She is, however, sympathetic to those she thinks need sympathy

Ophelia comes forward to make her first speech which she accompanies with strange and mannered hand movements

Ophelia   O, what a noble mind is here o'erthrown!
   The courtier's, soldier's, scholar's, eye, tongue, sword,
   Th'expectancy and rose of the fair state,
   The glass of fashion and the mould of form,
   Th'observed of all observers, quite, quite down!

She reaches a melodramatic pause

   *Eric enters from between the two flats. He is about forty, would-
   be sauve with a tendency to jaunty expression*

He eyes Ophelia appreciatively. She does not notice him

   And I, of ladies most deject and wretched,
   That sucked the honey of his —
Kate   (*from the back of the auditorium*) Eric!

Ophelia becomes instantly shy

Eric   (*out to Kate*) Hallo!
Kate   We're rehearsing, Eric!
Eric   So I see, Kate, love, but I thought you wanted me.

Kate begins to make her way towards the stage and Ophelia shrinks back to her place. As soon as Kate reaches the stage she advances on Eric

Kate   (*on the move*) Why must you come in through the set? You're the only one, Eric, the only one. Everyone else creeps in at the back of the hall if we've already started. Sometimes I don't even know if they're here till they're needed on stage.

Eric (*casually producing a slip of paper from a pocket*) But I thought I was needed. Ophelia and the Ghost, on stage, seven fifteen. It says so here.

Kate I know what it says; I wrote it myself. But it's nearly half-past and we can't sit around doing nothing for fifteen precious minutes. We have to be getting on with something!

Eric Yes. Sorry about that, Kate. I was —

Kate We're on in eight days, Eric. Eight days. You know what that means. You should be panicking.

Eric (*slipping an arm round her*) Look, it's going to be all right. You don't have to panic, you don't have to get tense. We're on course. I feel it in my bones.

Liz enters quickly from the wings. She carries the Ghost's costume

Liz Kate, did you want ...? (*She sees Eric and stops*) Oh.

Eric (*removing his arm*) Ah.

Kate sighs heavily

Liz, I wonder —

Liz (*coldly, deliberately cutting him*) Do you want him in costume, Kate?

Kate Please. If you don't mind.

Kate withdraws tactfully to speak to Ophelia. Liz sets the costume on a chair and starts to help Eric climb into it. There is a frosty silence for a while

Eric (*finally*) Liz, about last night —

Liz I'd rather not talk about it.

Eric Fine, fine. Whatever you say. (*He begins to whistle*)

Liz Do you mind?

Eric stops whistling

Eric Sorry. How did it go?

Liz How did it go?

Eric I was just wondering...

Liz You amaze me at times, Eric; you really do. The whole point about last night was that we were going to set things right with Mother. You were going to relax. You weren't going to try and impress her with smooth talk and flashy displays on her power mower this time.

Eric Flashy displays?

Liz One or two things were going to crop up very casually in the conversation. "I'm so sorry about the mower, Mrs Barker. Do let me buy you a new greenhouse. Liz and I are thinking of getting married, Mrs Barker. How do you feel about that?"

Eric All right, Liz. I know what I was supposed to say.

Liz Then where the hell were you?

Eric I was detained. I couldn't help it ——

Liz You weren't detained. You forgot!

Liz flings Eric's cloak down and storms off

Kate looks up, sees the disturbance and moves as if to follow Liz off. Eric smiles weakly at her

Kate Just put your cloak on, Eric.

Eric moves back and puts his cloak on. Before Kate can follow Liz, Ophelia trots up to her

Ophelia There was just one other thing. Did the business with the hands come over all right?

Kate The hands?

Ophelia Yes. I'm aware of this *tension* in Ophelia, you see, and I'm trying to bring it out by using my hands. (*She demonstrates her odd hand movements*)

Eric, his cloak now fixed, edges off after Liz

Kate Yes, I see. Do you think you could make them a little more subdued?

Ophelia Subdued?

Liz (*off*) Oh, go away!

Kate A little. The tension's coming quite nicely as it is, actually.

Eric shambles back on

(*Glancing at Eric*) Why don't you work on that speech, subduing the hands very slightly, while I go and check the costumes with Liz?

Kate goes off to see Liz

Ophelia begins to practise her hand movements and Eric, having seen that they are alone, comes up behind her

Eric That was sweet.

Ophelia Oh! Do you really think so?

Eric Absolutely. (*Indicating himself*) The corruption of the grave. (*Indicating Ophelia*) The sweet innocence of youth. Grown men will weep.

Ophelia Thanks very much.

Kate and Liz come back on

Eric and Ophelia are smiling at each other. At the sound of Liz's footsteps, Eric spins round and makes his way back to the chair where his clothes have been stacked. Liz intercepts him and hands him his hat with a piercing glance. She turns to Kate who is examining the pile of footwear DR. Ophelia returns to her chair

Liz He's more or less ready, Kate. And you're welcome to him.

Kate Don't take any notice of him. You know what he's like.

Liz (*unconvinced*) Perhaps.

Kate picks up the bag containing the boots

I hardly think it's the right time to mention those.

Kate   Oh yes it is. You leave it to me.

Liz   Really, Kate. Don't push it...

Kate   Leave it to me. You just go and see if Ophelia's all right.

Liz crosses back to Ophelia

Eric!

Eric   (*coming forward*) What's this?

Kate   You know what it is.

Eric   (*glancing in the bag*) No!

Kate   Eric...

Eric   No.

Kate   You've got to.

Eric   I am not wearing those boots.

Kate   Listen, Eric, the boots are dead right. I can just see you in——

Eric   No.

Kate   Will you let me finish? (*Pause*) Liz would like you to wear them.

Eric   I can't help that. They don't fit.

Kate   Then make them fit. This is very important to Liz. She wouldn't let anyone wear them, you know.

Eric   Sentimental nonsense.

Kate   For God's sake, Eric! They're her father's boots. Boots he wore on stage at Stratford. Doesn't that mean anything to you?

Eric   Of course it does. I love them like a brother. Like twin brothers to be precise. I just can't wear them.

Kate   You have worn them before. I know you have.

Eric   I'm sorry, Kate, but I don't think that you, as director, should even consider threatening my performance for the sake of sentiment.

Kate   Rubbish. They pinch a bit, that's all.

Eric   For the last time, no. (*He turns to go*)

Kate   (*a quiet threat*) I'll cut you out.

Eric   What?

Kate   I mean it; I'll do without you.

Eric   You can't. The Ghost? You can't.

Kate   I've thought about it. I'm quite prepared to record the Ghost as a voice-over.

Eric That's blackmail!

Kate Yes.

Eric (*after a slight pause*) They're not big enough.

Kate They'll fit.

Eric They'll hurt.

Kate Possibly.

Kate stares at Eric until he gives in and snatches the boots. As he bends to take them from the bag

(*Smiling, calling to Liz*) Trousers a bit baggy here, Liz. Can you do something? (*She moves back to Ophelia*)

Liz begins to fiddle with Eric's costume

Liz And what, may I ask, was that supposed to mean?

Eric What?

Liz Sweet!

Eric Sweet?

Liz (*mimicking*) That was sweet. Grown men will weep. Yeugh!

Eric It was a bit of encouragement, that's all.

Liz Encouragement! Huh! Grown men might weep. I nearly threw up.

Eric She was all right.

Liz I didn't mean her. I meant you.

Eric For goodness sake, Liz, what's got into you?

Liz Maybe I'm quaint and old-fashioned, Eric, but I find it a teeny bit upsetting when the eyes of the man I'm supposed to be engaged to are popping out with lust over a girl half his age.

Eric What do you mean by ——?

Liz You know very well what I mean by lust, Eric.

Eric It means absolutely nothing. She's just a sweet kid, that's all.

Liz There you are: sweet!

Eric What's wrong with that?

Liz (*popping out from behind him*) Sweet kids tend not to have what she's got that your eyes are popping out with lust over!

Eric You really do get yourself in a tangle when you're ratty, don't you?

Liz I am not ratty. I just happen not to like public displays of lust. (*She bobs down again and works away at Eric's trousers*)

Eric Will you stop going on about lust? I passed a paternalistic comment to a fellow actor; nothing more. I like to help people, Liz. I can't help that. OK, she's young and she's pretty ——

Liz suddenly takes in a particularly vicious tuck in Eric's costume

Ow! Go easy, Liz, for heaven's sake!

Liz No, Eric! You go easy. I'm warning you!

Liz goes

Eric watches ruefully and then notices the boots again. He picks them up gingerly and begins to squeeze into them. Kate comes over to him

Kate So, how are they?

Eric (*irritably*) Tight, Kate. As I said they'd be.

Kate I shouldn't worry. They'll probably mould themselves to your feet.

Eric I won't be able to walk in them though.

Kate You'll have to. There aren't any others. Besides, I'd like to use them. Not just because of Liz but because I think they'll bring something to the production.

Eric Corns probably.

Kate Oh for goodness sake stop griping! Why must you be so negative all the time? Now can we please get on with some work?

Eric All right, all right. No-one's keener than I am, you know.

Kate (*leaving the stage*) I'm going right to the back for this bit so will you please, please project?

Kate goes to the back of the auditorium and Ophelia approaches Eric tentatively as he examines his feet. She is shy and awed by him

Ophelia She's very good, isn't she?

Eric Kate?

Ophelia Well, Kate, yes, but I meant Liz, actually.

Eric Liz? She's all right, I suppose.

Ophelia Do you know what she just said to me?

Eric (*suddenly worried*) No. What?

Ophelia She said she was going to flatten my bust.

Eric She what?

Ophelia Flatten my bust. She said it was a bit too obvious and she didn't think Ophelia would be obvious in that kind of way. That's awfully good, isn't it?

Eric (*relieved*) Oh, yes. Awfully.

Ophelia It's so nice when the costumes people get involved at a textual level, don't you think?

Eric At the what?

Ophelia Textual level. You know: they're not simply dressing you up. They're much more ... well, involved.

Eric Oh yes. Liz is certainly that.

Ophelia She's going to put some tucks in it.

Eric In your bust?

Ophelia Yes. Well, in the dress.

Eric Oh good. (*Sidling closer*) Mind you, I don't think you're too obvious.

Ophelia Don't you really?

They are smiling at each other when Kate's voice comes at them from the auditorium

Kate Well, are we going to start or what?

Eric Sorry. Sorry, Kate. Er — who do you want first, the Ghost or Ophelia?

Kate The Ghost first, please. No words. I just want you to move in your costume. Come on as you do for the scene with Hamlet and Gertrude. Remember, you have a great weight of sin and anguish on your back. OK?

Eric A weight of sin. Right. Got it.

Eric exits gingerly

Ophelia retires to her chair to watch with intent interest. Nothing happens

Eric edges back on

(*To Kate*) Sorry?

Kate What?

Eric I didn't hear you.

Kate I didn't say anything.

Eric Oh sorry. I thought you were going to tell me when to start, that's all.

Kate No, Eric! Start when you're ready, please! There was really no need to go off.

Eric Oh. Would you rather I was back on again?

Kate No, no! Just carry on, and be quick about it. The others are due at eight.

Eric Right!

Eric gives Ophelia a quick smile and goes off again. After a slight pause he shoots back on as the ghost, hobbling in short painful steps

Kate Glide, please, Eric!

He glances resentfully in her direction and then continues - the same steps but slower

(*Beginning to rush towards the stage*) Glide ! Glide! You're supposed to be the Ghost for heaven's sake. You look more like something out of *The Mikado*!

Eric I'm sorry, Kate.

Kate Don't keep apologizing. Just try!

Eric You know what it is? It's these boots. I think I might be better off if I black up my plimsoles and wear them.

Kate (*storming on to the stage*) You are not wearing plimsoles in a production of mine. You are wearing those boots. Real actors go through all sorts of pain so surely you can put up with a couple of slightly pinched feet.

Eric Real actors? What do you mean by that?

Kate People who can act, Eric. That may include you. So far I have seen no evidence of it! Look, forget the Ghost for a moment. Hang on to the boots. Wear them in, all right? We'll go on to Ophelia. From where Hamlet leaves her, just before "O, what a noble mind ..." Right?

Eric . }
Ophelia } (*together*) Right.

Kate And instead of just standing there feeling sensitive about your feet, Eric, you can do Hamlet.

Eric perks up

Don't say anything.

He is deflated again

Just exit right, staring wildly into her eyes. Give her something to bounce off.

Eric (*perking up again*) Right. Fine. (*A quick look round*) Is Liz out there with you, Kate?

Kate No. You'll have to see her later.

Eric Oh well, never mind, never mind.

Kate May we proceed? OK? Just give me time to get to the back of the hall again.

Kate goes to the back of the hall and Ophelia approaches Eric

Ophelia Actually, I thought that was awfully good.

Eric What? What was?

Ophelia The way you walked. It certainly had something for me.

Eric Did it?

Ophelia Oh yes. It conveyed a — a broken quality, and that's as it should be, surely, because he was, in some ways, a broken man, wasn't he?

Eric Well, yes. He was. As I see him. Yes. (*Pause. He smiles at her*) I won't put you off, will I? Being here for this bit?

Ophelia Oh no, not at all. It'll be a great help, honestly.

Eric Something for you to bounce off.

Ophelia Exactly. It really will.

Eric Feel free to bounce off me any time you like.

They smile at each other before Kate calls out from the back of the auditorium

Kate Far be it from me to interrupt ...

Eric Yes! Sorry, Kate. From where Hamlet goes, right?

Kate Right!

Eric takes Ophelia's hands before, vastly overacting, staggering towards the wings. He then returns to clasp Ophelia again. With a quick look into the wings to make sure Liz is not lurking there, he moves in closer

Don't drool, Eric.

Eric What?

Kate Don't drool! We haven't got all night.

Eric You mean it was a bit too long?

Kate Just a shade, yes.

Eric OK, Kate. Fortissimo.

Kate What?

Eric Fortissimo. (*As if to a slow child*) With pace.

Eric returns to Ophelia, clutches her again, then begins to hobble off backwards looking pained and manic

Ophelia is gripped by this and, when Eric has eventually gone, blinks and cannot remember her words

Ophelia Sorry, Kate; it's gone. I know it perfectly well but it's just gone.

Kate (*charging back towards the stage*) "O, what a noble mind is here o'erthrown"! And it goes on to: "O, woe is me t'have seen what I have seen, see what I see". And you can say that again! Put the kettle on, someone. I must have some caffeine before the others turn up. And for goodness sake clear some of this mess up!

> *Kate gestures at some of the rehearsal clutter as she sweeps off. Ophelia follows anxiously*
>
> *Some Stage Hands enter, clear away the clutter and, under the direction of the Stage Manager, move a throne against one of the walls ready for Scene 2*

Scene 2

The same. Eight days later, after the first performance of Hamlet

Kate is sitting dejectedly on the throne

Eric enters without noticing her. He wears an outdoor coat and carries the bag containing the boots. He walks to the edge of the stage and stares out at the, for him, empty hall

Eric (*with cheerful resignation*) Oh well, you win some, you lose some. (*He turns to go and sees Kate. He is about to slip away before she notices him but thinks better of it and goes up to her*) Cheer up, Kate. I've known worse opening nights.
Kate Have you?
Eric Well, just as bad.
Kate They laughed, Eric. At *Hamlet*; they laughed.
Eric Yes ... well, that's not so bad. Bits of it are supposed to be funny. Comic relief.

Kate The duel, Eric? The deaths? The Ghost?

Eric Ah.

Kate To be perfectly honest, we could've done with some *tragic* relief, just to give them the chance to get their breath back; wipe their eyes before the next disaster set them off again.

Eric There were mistakes, granted, but when all's said and done it is only a play, isn't it?

Kate (*standing*) No, Eric. It is not only a play: it is *Hamlet*. Perhaps I should've done *Macbeth*. I mean that *is* supposed to be an unlucky play.

Eric Kate, Kate! What is all this, eh? (*Putting his arms round her*) You're letting things get on top of you, aren't you?

Kate (*pulling away*) Well I'm not letting you get on top of me, Eric, so you needn't think you can take advantage.

Eric Don't be silly. OK, so we had a bad first night. People have had bad first nights before and then gone on to great things. There are other nights, Kate.

Kate Two other nights.

Eric Yes, two other nights. Not much, but something.

Kate Twenty nights wouldn't be enough to wipe out the humiliation of tonight.

Eric Nonsense. One night is enough. So cut out all this *Macbeth* rubbish. There's no place for superstition in this game, in spite of what people say. I've been talking about *Macbeth* on and off all week and I don't suppose it's made the slightest difference.

Kate (*glaring at him*) I'm well aware what's wrong with this production. It all stems from a serious shortfall in the acting department. I feel I've been betrayed by people who ought to know better.

Eric By which you mean what?

Kate You know what I mean.

Eric No. Do tell me.

Kate (*decisively*) All right. There's an element of discord in the team, Eric, and a lot of it stems from the fact that you are endlessly mucking Liz about ——

Eric Kate! (*He turns away from her and takes out a cigarette and a lighter*)

Kate Liz is a friend of mine and I don't like to see it. You could say it's none of my business ——

Eric You're damn right it isn't. (*He flicks nonchalantly at the lighter which fails to work*)

Kate But when what you get up to begins to spoil my play I will not remain silent. Your heart's not in it, Eric. You're just not concentrating. (*Snatching at the lighter*) Will you stop fiddling with that thing! (*Slight pause*) The whole shambles of tonight stems from the hopelessness of your performance.

Eric (*after a thoughtful pause*) Are you not satisfied with the Ghost, Kate? Is this what you're trying to say?

Kate Well, there's no point trying to be polite now, is there? The Ghost is awful. Bloody awful. *You* are awful, Eric.

Eric All right, all right. I get the picture.

Kate So what are you going to do about it? Apart from patting my hand and telling me to cheer up.

Eric What am I going to do about it? I'm already doing what you've directed me to do. If the Ghost doesn't quite come off, Kate, you can put it simply and squarely down to one thing.

Kate What?

Eric Isn't it obvious?

It isn't

    (*Gesturing at the bag of boots*) Those boots!

Kate That's two things, Eric.

Eric You know it's true.

Kate Please don't give me all that stuff about the boots.

Eric It's not stuff. I'm totally inhibited by those boots. It's like having Liz's father looking over my shoulder all the time. And any way they hurt: they're giving me hell.

Kate You're a ghost. You're supposed to be in torment.

Eric (*brandishing the boots*) I cannot act in these!

Kate Those boots, Eric, have been worn by someone of talent and sensitivity. A real professional. Most people would jump at the chance to wear them.

Eric Well, I can't jump anywhere in them.

Kate You're making a fuss.

Eric And it doesn't surprise me the bloke was sensitive, in boots like these.

Kate Eric! This is ridiculous. You're being deliberately awkward. You know what they say, don't you? A bad workman always blames his tools.

Eric You really know how to hurt, don't you?

Kate Well, I'm sorry, but you didn't sit out there tonight and watch Marcellus and Barnardo brought down by a sliding tackle from behind. It was more like Fourth Division football than Shakespeare.

Eric But doesn't that exactly prove my point about the boots? They're not safe to wear.

Kate Oh shut up about the boots! If Liz's father could wear them in Stratford without felling everyone in sight —

Eric Stratford! You have no idea how sick I am of hearing you go on about Stratford. Stratford this; John Barton that; the RSC the other. You seem to think these bloody things are magic because they've had some fancy, famous face in them.

Kate Famous feet, Eric.

Eric Don't split hairs! You know very well what I mean! I do not give a monkey's who wore the things or whether Sir Laurence himself had his cocoa out of them. They do not fit properly. I do not like them! (*He throws them down*)

Pause

Kate (*a small sigh*) All right. Black up your plimsoles and wear them. Wear high heels for all I care. It's not going to make any difference now.

Eric (*snatching up the boots*) No! I shall wear the boots! (*He turns to go, stopping for the final word*) I have my pride. You'll see exactly what kind of a workman blames his tools, Kate!

Eric exits

Kate Rest, rest perturbed spirit.

Kate sniffs and goes off as the Stage Crew enter sombrely

They begin to take the walls down. They turn them round to make the rather shabby walls of the dressing-room. A door is fitted in the gap. It has a small window above it

Various bits of dressing-room paraphenalia are brought on: two small tables, a couple of chairs, a small mirror, some make-up, a skip of costume pieces etc. The Stage Crew exit through the door

Scene 3

The dressing-room. The following night

Ophelia enters and begins to practise her hand moves in front of a small mirror

Kate looks in and catches her at it

Ophelia (*embarrassed*) Oh. Hello.
Kate Is Eric here yet?
Ophelia I don't think so.
Kate If he turns up can you give me a call?
Ophelia If he turns up? Why shouldn't he turn up?
Kate No reason. I – I had a bit of a go at him last night, that's all. I don't think he took it very well.
Ophelia Oh, how awful. Do you think he won't turn up, then?
Kate I don't know. Yes, I'm sure he will. But he might be a bit tense.
Ophelia Can I help?
Kate I think not.
Ophelia Oh dear. Everyone seems tense tonight. You seem tense, Kate. You don't mind me saying that, do you?

Kate I don't mind. It's true enough. The hall is half full already.

Ophelia But that's good, isn't it?

Kate I'm not so sure. I think they've come for a laugh. Word's got round. You know, I nearly sneaked off to the pictures tonight. Who else is tense? Are you tense?

Ophelia Oh yes. Jolly tense. I'm tense most of the time, actually. I don't really know whether I'm more tense than usual or not. It's hard to tell. Liz is tense, I think. She just snapped at me.

Kate What for?

Ophelia I just asked her if my bust was all right and she was quite rude.

Kate You mentioned your bust? To Liz?

Ophelia Just in passing. I mean, I didn't make a big thing of it. Do you think I shouldn't have?

Kate Under the circumstances I don't think it was the most diplomatic subject to bring up.

Ophelia Really? Why?

Kate Well ... how shall I put this? It's to do with Eric.

Ophelia Eric? My bust? Good Lord, I should hope not. (*She laughs and looks down at her bust. She notices that Kate is not laughing and the penny drops*) Oh Kate, no.

Kate It does sometimes look as if you encourage him.

Ophelia But I don't. I mean, not in that way. I like him, of course, and he's very kind about my acting ...

Kate I don't think Liz would call it kindness.

Ophelia But, Kate, this is really terrible.

Kate Well, now you know you can be on your guard a bit.

Ophelia Oh Kate.

Kate I blame myself in part. I wanted you both coming from the back of the auditorium. Ophelia down one aisle: the innocence of youth. The Ghost down the other: the corruption of the grave. It would've been all right but it meant you had to use the same dressing-room.

Ophelia (*with a panicky look round*) Oh no!

Kate Liz did warn me. She said that by Saturday night you'd both be corrupt.

Ophelia What can I do, Kate?

Kate (*smiling*) Don't worry. He's not a monster. If you keep your distance, act a bit cool towards him, he'll soon get the message.

Ophelia Do you think so?

Kate Yes. And anyway Liz'll be around. You'll be safe. Don't think about Eric. Think about Ophelia.

Kate goes

Ophelia hurries to the mirror to examine her bust

Eric enters, whistling. He carries his trousers, coat, shoes etc., and is wearing the boots

Ophelia flies as far from him as she can

Eric (*sitting*) I'm sorry. Did I startle you? (*He arranges his belongings neatly in his corner*)

Ophelia No. Not at all.

Eric Good. You're all right, are you?

Ophelia (*coldly*) Yes, thank you. Quite all right.

Eric Good. (*It suddenly occurs to him why she is acting so strangely*) Kate's had a word with you, hasn't she?

Ophelia No. Well, what if she has? Which she hasn't.

Eric No? Then there must be some other reason for you cowering in the shadows like that. What did she say?

Ophelia I didn't say that she said anything.

Eric (*standing*) I'm entitled to know, I think.

Ophelia She said – she said you had your eye on me.

Eric (*laughing*) Is that all? Well, so I have.

Ophelia I don't think it'll do any good to deny it ... What?

Eric Of course I've had my eye on you. What's wrong with that?

Ophelia (*weakly*) I don't know really.

Eric Listen, you're a very attractive girl. You must realize that. Am I supposed to ignore the fact? (*He begins to edge closer to her*)

Ophelia Well ... I — I ...

Eric I like looking at beautiful paintings. I like looking at attractive girls. The one follows logically from the other. It doesn't mean that I have evil designs, does it? Liking beautiful paintings is not the same as liking to steal beautiful paintings.

He slips an arm round her shoulders while she still has her back to him but she scuttles away

Ophelia Well, no, it isn't, but ——

Eric Besides you're talented. That interests me too.

Ophelia (*turning back to him*) Talented?

Eric Don't pretend you don't know that either.

Ophelia Well, I am very keen.   (*During the following she edges a little closer*)

Eric I know dozens of people who are keen. I know only a very few who have genuine talent. You happen to be one of them. In my book that's exciting. (*He smiles*) So, are you telling me I shouldn't have noticed you, is that it?

Ophelia Oh dear. I don't know what to say now.

Eric Why do you think Kate had a word with you? To protect your interests, or hers?

Ophelia What do you mean?

Eric You must've noticed the way she's been treating me lately. Singling me out for special criticism. Making a great deal of fuss about little, unimportant things.

Ophelia Well, I suppose she has been rather heated lately. When she went on about your boots at the dress rehearsal ...

Eric The boots. Exactly. I mean, why make such a fuss about a pair of ridiculous boots that no-one is going to notice?

He smiles again and she smiles back and turns shyly away. He steps closer and winces as the boots nip his feet. She seems not to notice

If you think about it, it's not the boots; it's me.

Ophelia You?

Eric Yes. I don't like saying this about Kate. In many ways she's a fine person, and she has some good ideas, sometimes, but she is not you. She hasn't your looks or your talent, and she knows it, and she knows that I know it.

Ophelia You mean she's jealous?

Eric Who can say what jealousy is? She shouts. She says things she probably doesn't mean. OK, maybe that is jealousy.

Ophelia But you never say a thing in your defence. You make out it's the boots ...

Eric How can I shout back at her? How can I reveal the truth? Kate, you have neither the talent nor the beauty of this young girl here! (*He takes her by the shoulders*) It would be too cruel.

Ophelia Oh Eric, you are a very kind, a very caring person.

Eric Don't think too badly of her, will you?

Ophelia I'll try not to.

Eric And we're still friends?

Ophelia (*softly*) Oh yes. (*Nervously*) I mean, if you don't mind. I mean —

Eric (*stopping her lips with his fingers*) I don't mind.

He moves in for the clinch. She closes her eyes yieldingly. His cheap, hynoptic charm appears to be working but, before he can kiss her, he begins to breathe heavily and make snorting noises. He starts to stamp one leg like a bull. Ophelia opens her eyes. She backs off, puzzled. Groaning, he makes a lurch towards her and she bolts

Ophelia Don't! Don't come near me!

Ophelia runs out and slams the door

Eric (*hobbling after her*) No, wait. It's cramp. Come back. It's cramp! (*He hops around, sits, pulls off the boots and rubs his calves*) You buggers! You nasty-minded buggers! (*He throws the boots into the skip, slams down the lid and sits on it*)

Liz enters

Liz Eric! What have you been up to?

Eric I haven't been up to anything.

Liz What have you done to that girl?

Eric (*innocently*) Nothing.

Liz Nothing? Listen to me, Eric. She's just gone belting up the corridor like a frightened rabbit muttering that you're utterly disgusting. Stale news as far as I was concerned but it seemed like a revelation to her.

Eric I'm telling you, Liz, I've done nothing.

Liz "Nothing will come of nothing, Eric. Speak again."

Eric (*standing and moving to Liz*) Honestly, Liz, we were sitting in here, yards apart, not speaking, not even looking at each other, when suddenly I began to get this excruciating tingling in my calves.

Liz In your what?

Eric In my calves. The backs of my legs.

Liz I see.

Eric It was such agony I had to call out. I suppose it startled her.

Liz She was startled all right. You suddenly turned the full force of your greasy charm on her, didn't you? It's enough to startle anybody.

Eric It wasn't like that, Liz, honestly.

Liz If you say honestly once more, Eric, you'll feel an excruciating tingling somewhere else. Why don't you just tell the truth? The girl was simple enough to fall for your oily superficiality, you tried to go a bit too far a bit too soon and the old mask slipped. She suddenly saw you for what you are: a dirty old man!

Eric I am not old!

Liz Old, and ageing, and pathetic.

Eric You're not prepared to listen to a word I say, are you? I swear to you we were sitting here in absolute silence. I got cramp from your father's boots and —

Liz Oh, so it was Father's fault?

Eric I didn't say that.

Liz Then it must be the boots, mustn't it? Yes, of course. The boots are to blame. You sit there innocently humming to yourself while the boots tiptoe out of your bag and make their lascivious way towards the nubile creature you hardly noticed you were sharing a room with. Naughty, naughty boots. Why don't you face reality for once in your life? It's not the boots. It's you. You, Eric!

Eric Liz, honestly —

Liz (*shouting*) Forget it! (*Slight pause; quieter*) Forget me. You don't really want me, Eric. You want an admirer. Anyone will do.

Liz goes, slamming the door behind her

Eric Please, Liz! Listen to me. Listen to me! (*Pause. He sits dejectedly*)
Stage Hand (*off; calling from behind the closed door*) First call for the Ghost! Can we have the Ghost at the back of the hall in a couple of minutes, please!
Eric All right, all right! (*He stands and looks for the boots but can't find them*) Would you believe it? They've gone. (*He recalls throwing them in the skip, crosses to it and begins to search. His search becoming more and more desperate*) Come on. Come out, you nasty beggars... The show must go on... Come on. Don't be shy. Kate says you're the best things in it... Where the hell are you?
Stage Hand (*off; calling from behind the closed door*) Ghost now. Ghost to the back of the hall now, please!
Eric I can't! The bloody boots have walked! (*To the skip*) All right. Don't you say you haven't been warned. I'm going on without you. (*He goes to the door but it seems to be locked*) Liz? (*He rattles the handle*) Kate! (*He bangs on the door*) Hallo! I'm supposed to be on and I can't get out! (*He bangs more frantically*) Help! (*He looks round in desperation and sees the small window above the door. He grabs a chair and climbs on it. He fiddles with the catch and teeters*) Oh no!

Black-out

Help! Aargh!

In the Black-out Eric sprawls unconscious on the floor. The chair has fallen. The boots are placed DR in the position they were at the beginning of the play. A spotlight comes up on the boots, then the Lights come up on the dressing-room. Eric stirs and gets up painfully without noticing the boots. He sits on the skip, notices the boots, leaps up and stares from the boots to the skip. He then rushes back to his table to look at his watch

Good heavens! Eleven o'clock! It can't be *(He looks at the boots again)* You know what you've done now, don't you? You've made me miss the play. The whole bloody lot. And do you know what I'm going to do now? I'm going to take you for a little walk, down by the river, and I'm going to put you in a nice plastic bag – *(beginning to stuff the boots into a bag)* – with a nice little brick, and I'm going to throw you in! I don't care whose precious feet you —

He is interrupted by the door opening, slowly. He recalls that he was unable to open the door

  Ophelia enters

  (Instantly blustering) Listen. It wasn't what you thought it was: it was cramp.
Ophelia No. Please. Don't say anything. *(She walks up to Eric and kisses him)* Such pity, Eric. Can you forgive me for not understanding?
Eric For not understanding what?
Ophelia *(with a slow smile)* Everything. *(She is about to leave but hesitates at the door)* Any time, Eric. Any time.

  Ophelia goes

Eric is shocked and looks from her to the boots. He smiles

  Kate comes in. She is in a state of agitation

Kate Eric.
Eric *(jumping)* Kate! *(Backing away)* Look, I'm sorry, Kate. Deeply, deeply sorry —
Kate I don't think I can ever remember anything like it. It was harrowing!
Eric *(turning away from her and taking the boots from the bag)* You see, it was these bloody boots —
Kate Yes. I did tell you the boots were right, didn't I?
Eric I don't care what you say: there's something about them.

Kate Yes, yes. They ... I don't know... they seemed suspended.

Eric (*as if hearing her for the first time*) Suspended?

Kate Yes. You didn't seem to be walking. You were gliding.

Eric Gliding? You mean the Ghost glided?

Kate It set the whole tone. From the moment you came on the play was alive. It was beautiful, and harrowing. I came to say thank you.

Eric I came on?

Kate It was profoundly moving. You were so totally the Ghost that I didn't recognize you.

Eric No, I don't suppose you did.

Kate I'm sorry for what I said last night. I was under stress. You know I didn't mean it.

Eric That's all right, Kate. I can take it.

Kate smiles and makes to leave

Kate Oh, and Eric.

Eric Yes?

Kate Same again tomorrow night, OK?

Kate goes

Eric smiles wanly. He looks at the boots. His expression turns to one of horror and he throws them down. They land DR where Liz first placed them. The Lights fade to a spot on the boots

CURTAIN

FURNITURE AND PROPERTY LIST

Scene 1

On stage: Two chairs
Pots of paint
Pile of footwear
Coffee mugs
Coats
Cloth draped over flat

Off stage: Bag containing pair of boots (**Liz**)
Ghost's costume (**Liz**)

Personal: **Ophelia:** copy of *Hamlet*
Eric: slip of paper in pocket

Scene 2

On stage: Throne

Personal: **Eric:** cigarettes, lighter

Scene 3

On stage: Two tables. *On them:* **Eric**'s wristwatch,
make-up etc.
Two chairs
Small mirror
Skip containing costume items

Off stage: Trousers, coat, shoes etc. (**Eric**)

LIGHTING PLOT

Interior. A stage, a dressing-room. Practical fittings required: nil

To open: Dim lighting

Cue 1	Music *Bring up spot DR on pile of footwear*	(Page 1)
Cue 2	The music fades *Cross fade to general lighting*	(Page 1)
Cue 3	**Eric:** "On no!" *Black-out*	(Page 23)
Cue 4	When ready *Bring up spot on boots DR, then bring up* *general lighting on dressing-room*	(Page 23)
Cue 5	**Eric** throws the boots down *Fade to spot on boots DR*	(Page 25)

EFFECTS PLOT

Cue 1	When ready *Music*	(Page 1)
Cue 2	**Liz** leaves *Fade music*	(Page 1)